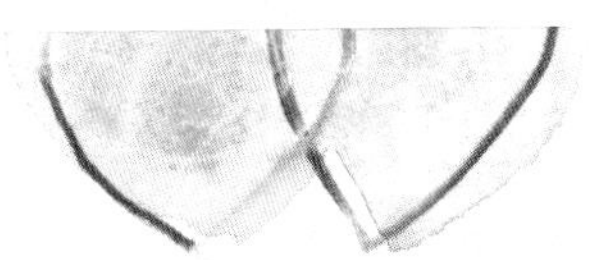

Published by
**Lion Publishing plc**
Sandy Lane West,
Oxford, England
www.lion-publishing.co.uk
ISBN 0 7459 4226 1
First edition 2000
10 9 8 7 6 5 4 3 2 1 0

**Acknowledgments**
10, 46: Song of Songs 8:7, I John 4:18, quoted from The New Revised Standard Version of the Bible, Anglicized Edition, copyright © 1989, 1995 by the Division of Christian Education of the National Council of the Churches of Christ in the United States of America, and used by permission. All rights reserved.
11: extract from 'As I Walked Out One Evening' by W.H. Auden, copyright © Faber & Faber Ltd. Used by permission.
18, 60: Mark 10:6–8, Galatians 6:2, quoted from the Good News Bible published by The Bible Societies/HarperCollins Publishers Ltd, UK © American Bible Society 1966, 1971, 1976, 1992, used with permission.
21: extract from *The Alternative Service Book, 1980*, copyright © The Archbishops' Council and reproduced by permission.
35: extract from *The Methodist Service Book*, copyright © Trustees for Methodist Church Purposes and used by permission of Methodist Publishing House.
Every effort has been made to trace and acknowledge copyright holders of all the quotations in this book. We apologize for any errors or omissions that may remain, and would ask those concerned to contact the publishers, who will ensure that full acknowledgment is made in the future.
A catalogue record for this book is available from the British Library
Typeset in 11/15 Elegant Garamond
Printed and bound in Singapore

Compiled by Sarah Hall

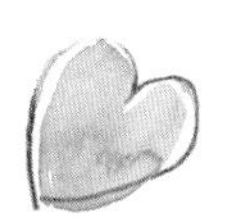

# *Taking the plunge*

*Here are some words of wisdom and celebration for your special day. Of course it will all go by in a blur of excitement, nerves, greetings, solemn moments and joyful ones.*

*Yet it marks the beginning of a great adventure as you begin your life together. May the adventure of marriage be an exciting and enriching experience for you both.*

# Love and Marriage

*Many waters cannot quench love,*
*neither can floods drown it.*

FROM THE OLD TESTAMENT SONG OF SONGS

*I'll love you, dear, I'll love you*
*Till China and Africa meet,*
*And the river jumps over the mountain*
*And the salmon sing in the street.*

W.H. Auden

*If ever two were one, then surely we.*
*If ever man were loved by wife,*
*then thee;*
*If ever wife was happy in a man,*
*Compare with me, ye women,*
*if you can.*

*Thy love is such I can no way repay,*
*The heavens reward thee manifold,*
*I pray.*
*Then while we live, in love let's so*
*persever*
*That when we live no more, we may*
*live ever.*

ANNE BRADSTREET

*Where love rules, there is no will to power, and where power predominates, love is lacking. The one is the shadow of the other.*

C.G. Jung

*Love seeketh not itself to please,*
*Nor for itself hath any care,*
*But for another gives its ease,*
*And builds a Heaven in Hell's despair.*

William Blake

# What It's All About

*Jesus said, 'In the beginning,*
*at the time of creation, "God*
*made them male and female,"*
*as the scripture says. "And for this*
*reason a man will leave his father*
*and mother and unite with his*
*wife, and the two will become one."*
*So they are no longer two, but one.'*

FROM THE NEW TESTAMENT GOSPEL OF MARK

*I sing of brooks,*
*of blossoms,*
*birds, and bowers:*
*Of April, May,*
*of June, and July-flowers.*
*I sing of Maypoles, Hock-carts,*
*wassails, wakes,*
*Of bridegrooms, brides, and of their*
*bridal cakes.*

ROBERT HERRICK

*Marriage is like
twirling a baton,
turning handsprings, or
eating with chopsticks;
it looks easy till you try it.*

HELEN ROWLAND

*Marriage is given, that husband and wife may comfort and help each other, living faithfully together in need and in plenty, in sorrow and in joy.*

The Alternative Service Book

*Hail, wedded love,
mysterious law, true source
Of human offspring.*

John Milton

*The married state, with and without the affection suitable to it, is the completest image of heaven and hell we are capable of receiving in this life.*

RICHARD STEELE

*Ven you're a married man, Samivel, you'll understand a good many things as you don't understand now; but vether it's worth while goin' through so much to learn so little, as the charity-boy said ven he got to the end of the alphabet, is a matter o' taste.*

CHARLES DICKENS

*Marrying a man is like buying something you've been admiring for a long time in a shop window. You may love it when you get it home, but it doesn't always go with everything else in the house.*

JEAN KERR

*I learned a long time ago that the only people who count in any marriage are the two that are in it.*

HILLARY RODHAM CLINTON

*Like everything which is not the involuntary result of fleeting emotion but the creation of time and will, any marriage, happy or unhappy, is infinitely more interesting than any romance, however passionate.*

W.H. AUDEN

*Marriage, says the Christian, is for life; and the wedding is a declaration that it is so. It is a fearsome declaration to make, and without the grace of God, arrogant and absurd.*

HAROLD LOUKES

*Like fingerprints, all marriages are different.*

George Bernard Shaw

Living
Together

*With this Ring I thee wed, with my body I thee worship, and with all my worldly goods I thee endow.*

THE BOOK OF COMMON PRAYER

*One man should love
and honour one:
A bride-bed
Theirs alone till life's done.*

EURIPIDES

*My Love in her attire doth show her wit,*
*It doth so well become her:*
*For every season she hath dressings fit,*
*For winter, spring and summer.*
*No beauty she doth miss,*
*When all her robes are on:*
*But Beauty's self she is,*
*When all her robes are gone.*

AUTHOR UNKNOWN

*We pray for this couple, that in their marriage all your will for them may be fulfilled; bestow upon them the gift and heritage of children; and endue them with all the gifts and graces needed for wise parenthood; through Jesus Christ our Lord. Amen.*

THE METHODIST SERVICE BOOK

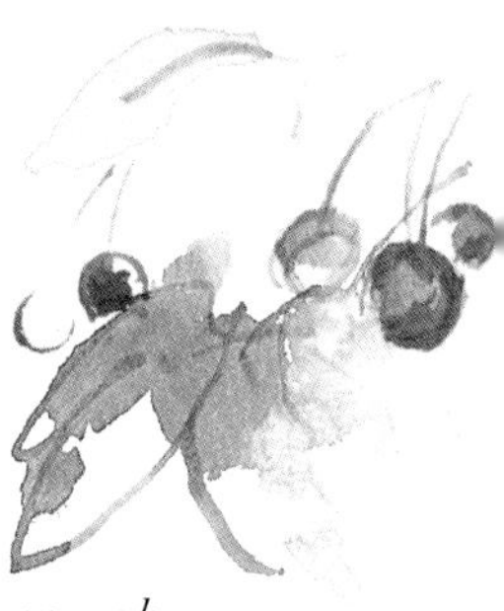

*Who of us is mature enough for offspring before the offspring themselves arrive? The value of marriage is not that adults produce children but that children produce adults.*

Peter De Vries

*True Love is but a humble,*
*low-born thing,*
*And hath its food served up*
*in earthen ware;*
*It is a thing to walk with, hand in hand,*
*Through the everydayness of this*
*workday world.*

J.R. Lowell

*The fulfilment of marriage is that joy in which each lover's true being is flowering because its growth is being welcomed and unconsciously encouraged by the other in the infinite series of daily decisions which is their life together.*

J. Neville Ward

*Except thou build it, Father,*
*The house is built in vain,*
*Except thou, Saviour, bless it,*
*The joy will turn to pain;*
*But nought can break the marriage*
*Of hearts in thee made one,*
*And love thy Spirit hallows*
*Is endless love begun.*

JOHN ELLERTON

# Wise Words

*Never marry but for love; but see that thou lovest what is lovely.*

William Penn

*Marriage is an adventure because our hearts know more than our minds.*

MIKE YACONELLI

*In marriage do thou be wise: prefer the person before money, virtue before beauty, the mind before the body; then thou hast a wife, a friend, a companion, a second self.*

William Penn

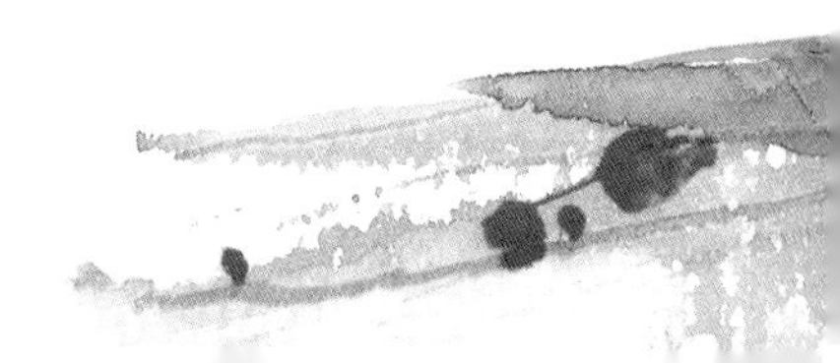

*More belongs to marriage than four legs in a bed.*

THOMAS FULLER

*There is no fear in love, but perfect love casts out fear.*

FROM THE NEW TESTAMENT FIRST LETTER OF JOHN

*O! beware, my lord, of jealousy;*
*It is the green-eyed monster*
*which doth mock*
*The meat it feeds on.*

WILLIAM SHAKESPEARE

*Often the difference between a successful marriage and a mediocre one consists of leaving about three or four things a day unsaid.*

HARLAN MILLER

*No marriage can
survive without
the words 'I'm sorry.'
No 'I'm sorry' can
survive without a
change of behaviour.*

MIKE YACONELLI

# No Longer Two, but One

*There is no more lovely, friendly and charming relationship than a good marriage.*

MARTIN LUTHER

*The meeting of*
*two personalities*
*is like the contact of*
*two chemical substances:*
*if there is any reaction,*
*both are transformed.*

C.G. JUNG

*Between husband and wife… all things should be in common, without any distinction or means of distinguishing.*

MARTIN LUTHER

*When a match has equal partners*
*then I fear not.*

Aeschylus

*In true marriage lies*
*Nor equal, nor unequal. Each fulfils*
*Defect in each, and always thought*
*in thought,*

*Purpose in purpose, will in will,*
*they grow,*
*The single pure and perfect animal,*
*The two-celled heart beating,*
*with one full strike,*
*Life.*

ALFRED, LORD TENNYSON

*A good marriage is that in which each appoints the other guardian of his solitude.*

RAINER MARIA RILKE

*Let there be spaces in your togetherness.*

KAHLIL GIBRAN

*Help to carry one another's burdens, and in this way you will obey the law of Christ.*

FROM THE NEW TESTAMENT
LETTER TO THE GALATIANS

*No human relation gives one possession in another – every two souls are absolutely different. In friendship or in love, the two side by side raise hands together to find what one cannot reach alone.*

KAHLIL GIBRAN